LANGUAGE ARTS EXPLORER

# MOTION AND FORCES

by Rebecca Hirsch

SCIENCE LAB:
MOTION AND FORCES

CHERRY LAKE PUBLISHING • ANN ARBOR, MICHIGAN

Published in the United States of America
by Cherry Lake Publishing
Ann Arbor, Michigan
www.cherrylakepublishing.com

Printed in the United States of America
Corporate Graphics Inc
September 2011
CLFA09

**Consultants:** Peter Barnes, assistant scientist, University of Florida; Gail Saunders-Smith, associate professor of literacy, Beeghly College of Education, Youngstown State University

Editorial direction:        Design and production:
Lisa Owings                 Craig Hinton

**Photo credits:** Paul Topp/Dreamstime, cover, 1; Dreamstime, 5; AP Images, 7; Levent Konuk/Shutterstock Images, 8; Aspen Photo/Shutterstock Images, 11; Richard Paul Kane/ Shutterstock Images, 13; Fotolia, 14 (inset); Shutterstock Images, 14, 20; Ljupco Smokovski/ Shutterstock Images, 16; Jarvis Gray/Shutterstock Images, 19; Victor Burnside/Dreamstime, 23; Brett Mulcahy/Shutterstock Images, 24; Mana Photo/Shutterstock Images, 27

**Library of Congress Cataloging-in-Publication Data**
Hirsch, Rebecca E.
 Science lab. Motion and forces / by Rebecca Hirsch.
    p. cm. – (Language arts explorer. Science lab)
 Includes index.
 ISBN 978-1-61080-205-5 – ISBN 978-1-61080-294-9 (pbk.)
 1. Force and energy–Juvenile literature. 2. Motion–Juvenile literature. I. Title. II. Title: Motion and forces.
 QC73.4.H57 2011
 531'.6–dc23

                              2011015130

**Cherry Lake Publishing would like to acknowledge the work of The Partnership for 21st Century Skills. Please visit www.21stCenturySkills.org for more information.**

# TABLE OF CONTENTS

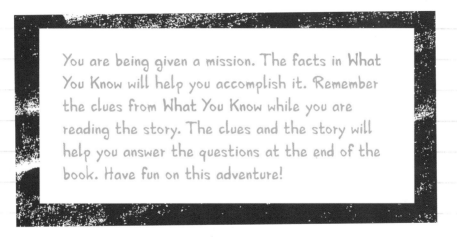

You are being given a mission. The facts in What You Know will help you accomplish it. Remember the clues from What You Know while you are reading the story. The clues and the story will help you answer the questions at the end of the book. Have fun on this adventure!

You can't see forces, yet nothing happens without them. Forces are pushes or pulls, and they make objects move in different ways. Your mission is to investigate forces and how they create motion. What forces do you make? What forces are at work on you? How do forces affect the motion of cars, baseballs, bicycles, surfboards, and roller coasters? Read the facts in What You Know and start learning about the dynamic world of motion and forces.

## WHAT YOU KNOW

★ Matter is anything you can touch—wood, water, grass, metal, and even air. All matter is made of tiny particles called **molecules**.

★ Mass is the amount of matter in an object. A heavy object has a greater mass than a light object.

★ Forces are the pushes and pulls that act on people and objects. You can't see forces, but you can feel them.

The Kingda Ka is the world's tallest roller coaster. How fast do you think it can go?

★ Speed tells us how fast an object is moving. It is the distance traveled in a certain period of time, such as miles per hour or feet per second.

★ **Acceleration** is a change in speed. It happens when an object slows down, speeds up, or changes direction.

Chloë Reynolds is a reporter from *ScienceFUN* magazine. She is part of a team that has been sent to investigate motion and forces. Carry out your mission by reading her journal.

We start our investigation in Minnesota with a visit to Dr. Bob MacAllister. He is an automotive engineer, a scientist who designs cars. He walks us through the big garage that is his laboratory.

"The first thing you need to learn about motion is something called **inertia**," says Dr. MacAllister. "Inertia means that an object that is not moving will not start moving by itself. It will stay at rest. Inertia also means that a moving object will not stop, speed up, or change direction unless something makes it. Anytime you see something change its speed or direction, you can be sure there is a force behind it."

## NEWTON'S LAWS

In 1687, Isaac Newton presented the three laws of motion he'd discovered. Inertia is Newton's first law of motion. Newton's second law says the amount of force needed to move an object depends on the mass of that object and the object's acceleration. Newton's third law says that when an object is pushed, that object pushes back with equal force. When you walk, your foot pushes against the ground, and the ground pushes back with equal force on your foot.

Inertia can be deadly in a car accident. Seat belts and air bags safely stop your body from moving forward.

We learn from Dr. MacAllister that inertia governs the way all objects move. If you place a soccer ball on the floor, it will not move unless something pushes or pulls it. The ball has inertia.

We are curious to learn more. How do scientists know that an object will keep moving unless something acts on it?

Dr. MacAllister takes us for a car ride to show us inertia in action. After we've been driving for a while, he says, "Right now we are cruising along at about 30 miles per hour (50 kmh). This car has inertia and so does your body. That means you and the car will both keep moving at this speed. But what happens if I accelerate to 50 miles per hour (80 kmh)?" He steps on the gas, and we feel our backs press into our seats. "Your body will keep moving at the slower speed until the car seat forces you forward. You feel as if you are pushed back against the seat. The reason is inertia." We keep speeding along until a traffic light in front of us turns yellow.

"Let's see what happens when I step on the brakes," says Dr. MacAllister. We giggle as we are all thrown forward against our seat belts. "As you noticed, your body keeps moving along at the faster speed until something stops it. In this case, that something was your seat belt.

brake pad assembly

rotor

Cars use friction to slow down or stop. The brake pads rub against the rotors.

"The situation can become dangerous when you are in a car going fast, and the car suddenly collides with something. Your body will keep going until something stops it. If you are not wearing a seat belt, that something could be the windshield. But a seat belt protects you, safely stopping your body from continuing forward." I tighten my seat belt a little.

Back at the garage, Dr. MacAllister tells us that he is working on designing better brakes for cars. Brakes work by using friction. Friction is the force created when two things rub together. When the driver hits the brakes, pads come down to squeeze against the wheels' rotors. Friction between the brake pads and the rotors slows the car down.

Cars also need friction to speed up. Friction between the tires and the road helps get the car moving. Friction even helps us walk. Think of trying to walk or run on slippery ice, and you'll realize how important friction is for helping us stay on our feet. ★

Today we are at a Major League Baseball training camp in Florida. We are talking with Mr. Gary DeLuca, who helps the players train. Nearby, a pitcher hurls balls into a catcher's mitt.

Mr. DeLuca tells us that baseball is a game of motion and forces. He points to the pitcher. "See how he starts with his weight back? Then he steps forward and uses a whiplike motion of his arm. The pitcher is applying force to the ball. He transfers energy from his body to the ball."

We learn that many forces affect the ball's motion. The strength of the pitcher's throw is one force. Another force is called drag, and it comes from air pushing on the ball and slowing it down. One part of drag is friction, which is created when the surface of the ball rubs against the air molecules surrounding it.

Mr. DeLuca pulls a baseball out of his coat pocket. "See the red stitches that hold the ball together? They are more than just decoration." He tells us that the stitches change the way the ball interacts with the air around it. The stitches cut down on the force the ball needs to push the air out of the way. Without the stitches, the ball wouldn't be able to slice through the air as fast.

Pitchers use their entire bodies to apply force to the ball.

We learn that how the pitcher throws the ball is important too. By changing the way he holds and throws the ball, a pitcher can give the ball spin. Spin changes the way air flows around the ball. If the pitcher wants to throw a fastball, he lets the ball roll off his fingers with a little backward spin. The fastest pitchers can throw the ball more than 100 miles per hour (160 kmh).

If a pitcher wants to throw a curveball, he throws the ball with a snapping, wrist-twisting motion. This gives the ball a forward spin as it flies through the air. The spin gives the curveball a crazy path, making it drop at the end. Curveballs are very hard to hit.

Next, Mr. DeLuca points to the catcher, who squats with his mitt as the pitcher fires balls at him. "The catcher has a difficult job," says Mr. DeLuca. "He must anticipate where the ball is going to go and stop it instantly, absorbing the force of the ball with his hand and glove."

We walk over to the batting cages, where some players are practicing their swings. I ask Mr. DeLuca how batters use motion and forces. He tells us that the batter must predict very quickly where the ball is going to go. If he guesses right, he might get a hit. If he guesses wrong—strike!

When the batter swings, he transfers energy from his body to the bat. The bat hits the ball with a huge amount of force. The force is so great that the bat and ball both change shape: the bat flexes, and the ball is pressed flat. In that

## ENERGY AT BAT

The kind of bat makes a big difference when hitting a baseball. Aluminum bats are better at transferring their energy to the ball. In Major League Baseball, only wooden bats are allowed. Aluminum bats would make it too easy to hit a home run!

A batter has less than half a second to decide whether to try hitting the ball.

instant, the bat transfers much of its energy to the ball, sending the ball sailing through the air with great speed. Just how fast and far the ball will travel depends on many factors. Batters use the factors they can control to try to hit the ball out of the park. ★

Our next stop is the ProCycle Factory in Tennessee, where we talk with bicycle designer Andrea Moreau. Ms. Moreau has been designing bicycles for 25 years.

As we walk around her factory, we see many different kinds of bikes. I ask Ms. Moreau what goes into designing a bicycle. She tells us the first thing to consider is what kind of riding you want to do.

"Some people like to ride on mountains and rough trails," she says. She shows us a purple bike with a thick

Mountain bikes have wide, rough tires that create friction with the road.

One of the first things any cyclist must learn is balance. Gravity is a natural force that pulls objects toward Earth. A bicyclist overcomes gravity by lifting his body above the earth's surface and balancing it on the bicycle. He must keep his weight directly above the base of the bicycle. If his body tilts too far to one side, he falls. Early bicyclists perched high above a gigantic wheel, an efficient design for going fast. But it was very dangerous. If the cyclist lost his balance, he had a long way to fall.

frame and fat tires. "This is a mountain bike. It has fat tires, and they are inflated to be a little squishy." Fat, squishy tires are good for riding on bumpy dirt roads. Their rough, knobby surfaces grip the trail. Friction between the tires and the road helps prevent slips and falls.

"But other people want to race on smooth roads. They need a bike that is built for speed." She shows us a racing bicycle that she designed. It has a thin, light frame and skinny tires. I give the tire a squeeze and feel how firm it is. Ms. Moreau explains that a thin, well-inflated tire doesn't squash as much against the road. This creates less friction because there is less tire rubbing against the road's surface. By keeping friction low, the rider can go faster.

Bicyclists can reduce wind resistance by changing the shape of their bodies.

She tells us that another problem for bicycle designers is wind resistance, the force of air pushing against the cyclist. The faster a rider goes, the more wind resistance there is to overcome. In a race, a cyclist has to work hard to push through the air.

Ms. Moreau explains that bicycle designers are always experimenting to create bicycles that overcome wind resistance. The goal is to create **aerodynamic** shapes, ones that slice through the air efficiently. But this isn't always easy. For instance, a solid wheel with no spokes is more aerodynamic, but it is also heavier and harder to pedal.

"But the biggest obstacle," Ms. Moreau tells us, "is the human body. Our bodies are just not made to sail through the air at high speeds." When a bicyclist is upright, his body has to push a larger mass of air out of the way, creating more wind resistance. Racing bicycles have special handlebars so that riders can lean forward and tuck in their arms, reducing wind resistance.

Then Ms. Moreau shows us another bicycle design. It is called a recumbent bike. "It looks strange to people who are used to the traditional kind," she says, "but it is a very smart design." She climbs on board and pedals with her legs out in front of her. Because she sits low to the ground and lies back, there is much less wind resistance. Less of her body faces the air, so a smaller mass of air has to be pushed aside for her to move forward. Recumbent bicycles are so efficient that they are banned in many races because traditional bicycles might not be able to compete against them. ★

We have come to the Hawaiian island of Maui. Helping us today is Ms. Julia Kaui, a lifelong surfer and surfing instructor.

When we arrive at the beach, Ms. Kaui is in the ocean on her surfboard, waiting for a wave. We watch her paddle hard as the wave comes up behind her. As the wave begins to push her forward, she stands up with her knees bent and her arms out. She flashes us a smile as she glides toward us. When her ride is over, she tips back into the water. A few seconds later, we see her hanging onto the back of her board and giving us a thumbs-up.

## TIDES

One of the forces surfers have to watch for comes from the moon. The moon's gravity tugs on the earth and creates tides. Because water flows and can move about easily, the oceans are pulled by the moon's gravity. The water is deeper at high tide and shallower at low tide. Surfers know there is usually some point in the tide cycle when the water is just right for surfing, and that is when they hit the beach.

Surfers have to paddle hard to catch the wave before it starts to break.

Once Ms. Kaui is back on shore, she tells us that surfing is all about balancing forces. "When a surfer is waiting on her board on top of the water," she says, "two forces are at play. They are gravity and buoyancy." Gravity pulls the surfer downward. Buoyancy holds her up. Buoyancy is the force of the water pushing up on the board and the surfer.

Ms. Kaui says that balancing these forces is a tricky thing, even in still water, and it is one of the first lessons a new surfer must learn. If gravity and buoyancy are balanced, then the surfer floats on the water. A surfer must always pay attention to her center of gravity, her balance point on the board. If she shifts her weight, she changes the balance. She can tip the board up or down or twist it to the side.

When a wave comes, there is a new force in play— the wave itself. Moving with the wave while balancing on the board takes a lot of skill. When the surfer sees a wave coming, she starts paddling forward, accelerating to match the speed of the wave. As the wave pushes her forward, she stands on the board. By keeping her knees bent and her arms out, she constantly adjusts her balance. As the wave starts to break, she shifts her weight to turn left or right, depending on which way the wave is breaking.

By shifting their weight, surfers can control the way their board cuts through a wave.

Ms. Kaui explains that there is yet another force a surfer has to worry about, and that is the force of the water dragging against the surfboard. This is friction again, and it slows her down. Ms. Kaui turns over her board and shows us the bottom. It looks glossy and smooth. She says this helps to cut down on friction. The top of the board is rough to give the surfer more control. A rudder at the back of the board keeps it from slipping sideways in the water.

"When you ride a wave," says Ms. Kaui, "you are using the force of the moving water to power your ride." As the water pushes the surfer faster and faster, she can shift her weight to ride high or low on the wave. She might lose a little speed as she climbs the wave, but she can gain it back by letting gravity pull her down again. ★

It is the last day of our investigation, and we have decided to spend it at an amusement park in Ohio. This place is all about motion and forces. All around the park, rides are pulling, spinning, whirring, and swinging.

We are here to ride the park's brand new roller coaster. It seems everyone wants to ride it. Waiting in line, I joke around and try to look calm. But my insides are squirming. I hear screams from overhead, and I look up as the roller coaster shoots down a huge hill.

Finally, it is our turn to ride. We sit in the front row and pull down a padded bar that locks across our bodies, holding us tight. When all the riders are ready, the car lurches forward. We climb the first hill. At the top,

## SUPER COASTERS

For some thrill seekers, gravity-powered coasters just aren't fast enough. Roller coaster engineers came up with a way to meet this need for speed. The technology they developed can launch riders to speeds of more than 120 miles per hour (193 kmh) in seconds! Kingda Ka riders rocket to 128 miles per hour (206 kmh) in just 3.5 seconds.

A roller coaster zooms down the lift hill as fast as gravity can pull it. Inertia keeps it going until the end of the ride.

there is a pause and then, whoosh! We fly down the hill, race up the next one, and spin around and around through a sideways loop. I scream the entire time.

Afterward, we talk to Mr. Ryan Liebling, one of the engineers who designed this roller coaster. We ask him about the forces that make this exciting ride go. Mr. Liebling tells us a roller coaster is not powered by an engine. A chain pulls the car to the top of the first hill. When the car is released, gravity takes over.

"The first hill is called the lift hill, and it is always the biggest," he says. "The force that powers the ride is gravity. As the roller coaster car climbs that first hill, it must work

As riders fly around curves and through loops, they experience centripetal force.

against gravity. Then the car rolls over the top, and gravity pulls it faster and faster. Inertia keeps the car going as it races up the next hill, and then gravity takes over again, and the car zooms downhill. The hills gradually become smaller as the ride goes along. Finally, as the car nears the end of the ride, the brakes are applied, and the car lurches to a stop."

We ask Mr. Liebling what sorts of things an engineer has to keep in mind when designing a roller coaster.

"The first thing is to make it fun," he tells us. "What makes a roller coaster exciting is the way your body is pushed and pulled. Curves are really fun." We learn that when you go around a curve, something called centripetal force is acting on your body. Inertia makes your body want to continue traveling in a straight line. Centripetal force keeps you moving on a circular path. When you feel your body lean to the outside of the car, centripetal force is what pushes inward. The faster you go around the curve, and the tighter the loop, the greater the centripetal force.

Mr. Liebling says roller coaster engineers balance the size of each hill and the shape of the loops so the car has enough energy to get through the entire ride. They carefully consider the size and steepness of each hill so the roller coaster doesn't go dangerously fast. It is important to make the ride exciting and scary, but never dangerous. Roller coasters use the laws of motion and forces to make you feel like you are in danger, even though you are not. ★

Congratulations! You have learned a lot about how motion and forces work. You've learned about Isaac Newton's laws of motion. You've learned how these laws apply to the motion of cars, baseballs, bicycles, surfboards, and roller coasters. You've discovered how forces affect motion. You've discovered that forces such as friction, gravity, and wind resistance can slow motion down. You've learned how forces can power a surfboard or a roller coaster. Congratulations on a mission well done!

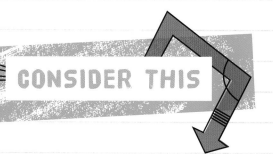

## CONSIDER THIS

★ If you place a book on the floor, it will not move. How does inertia explain this observation? What forces are at work if you push the book off the edge of a table?

★ A bicyclist is out for a ride. What two forces might slow her down?

★ What are some strategies a baseball pitcher uses to transfer energy from his body to the ball?

What forces might be acting on this surfer as he catches some air?

★ A boat floats on a lake. What two forces must be balanced for the boat to stay afloat?

★ What powers a roller coaster as it rolls up and down hills?

**acceleration (ak-sel-uh-RAY-shun)** a change in speed or direction

**aerodynamic (air-oh-dye-NAM-mik)** streamlined to move efficiently through the air, minimizing wind resistance

**centripetal force (sen-TRIP-uh-tuhl FORSS)** the force that keeps an object moving on a circular path

**friction (FRIK-shuhn)** a force created when two objects rub against each other; friction slows down objects that are moving

**inertia (in-UR-shuh)** the tendency for an object to stay at rest or in motion unless something acts on it

**molecule (MAH-luh-kyool)** the smallest particle of a material that has the same properties as that material

**wind resistance (WIND ri-ziss-tuhnss)** the force created when a mass of air pushes against a moving object; wind resistance is also called drag

## LEARN MORE

### BOOKS

Gardner, Robert. *Forces and Motion Science Fair Projects: Using the Scientific Method.* Berkeley Heights, NJ: Enslow, 2010.

Hollihan, Kerry Logan. *Isaac Newton and Physics for Kids: His Life and Ideas with 21 Activities.* Chicago: Chicago Review Press, 2009.

Koll, Hilary, Steve Mills, and Korey T. Kiepert. *Using Math to Design a Roller Coaster.* Milwaukee, WI: Gareth Stevens, 2007.

Mercer, Bobby. *The Leaping, Sliding, Sprinting, Riding Science Book: 50 Super Sports Science Activities.* New York: Lark Books, 2006.

### WEB SITES

Amusement Park Physics

http://www.learner.org/interactives/parkphysics/index.html

Learn about motion and forces at an amusement park and design your own roller coaster.

Science of Cycling

http://www.exploratorium.edu/cycling/index.html

Learn how professional cyclists use science to win races.

## PAPER AIRPLANE RACES

You can do this activity by yourself or with a friend. Make a few different paper airplanes. You can design your own or try one of the designs at http://www.10paperairplanes.com. Grab a timer and a tape measure and find a wide-open space with little or no wind. Launch the first paper airplane. How long does it stay in the air? How far does it go? Try each airplane. Which design performs the best? Experiment with different kinds of paper and different designs. What happens if you attach a paper clip to the airplane's nose?

## INERTIA IN ACTION

Make a ramp using a board and a stack of books. Slant the board by placing the stack of books under one end. Place another stack of books at the lower end of the ramp creating a barrier for anything that rolls down the ramp. Find a toy car or truck and balance a block, eraser, or other light object on it. Let the car roll down the ramp and crash into the barrier. What happens to the small object when the car collides with the barrier?

# INDEX

## ABOUT THE AUTHOR

Rebecca Hirsch holds a PhD from the University of Wisconsin-Madison and worked as a scientist before becoming a writer. She loves playing baseball, bicycling, and riding roller coasters but has never been on a surfboard. She lives with her husband and three children in State College, Pennsylvania.

## ABOUT THE CONSULTANTS

Peter Barnes has always been fascinated by energy and matter in space. For the past 25 years, he has been studying how stars form in the Milky Way, our home galaxy. He lives in Gainesville, Florida, with his wife and two science-loving children.

Gail Saunders-Smith is a former classroom teacher and Reading Recovery teacher leader. Currently she teaches literacy courses at Youngstown State University in Ohio. Gail is the author of many books for children and three professional books for teachers.